SUPER RATS

by Karen Latchana Kenney

Ideas for Parents and Teachers

Pogo Books let children practice reading informational text while introducing them to nonfiction features such as headings, labels, sidebars, maps, and diagrams, as well as a table of contents, glossary, and index.

Carefully leveled text with a strong photo match offers early fluent readers the support they need to succeed.

Before Reading

• "Walk" through the book and point out the various nonfiction features. Ask the student what purpose each feature serves.

• Look at the glossary together. Read and discuss the words.

Read the Book

• Have the child read the book independently.

• Invite him or her to list questions that arise from reading.

After Reading

• Discuss the child's questions. Talk about how he or she might find answers to those questions.

• Prompt the child to think more. Ask: What did you know about rats before you read this book? What more do you want to learn after reading it?

Pogo Books are published by Jump!
5357 Penn Avenue South
Minneapolis, MN 55419
www.jumplibrary.com

Library of Congress Cataloging-in-Publication Data

Names: Kenney, Karen Latchana, author.
Title: Super rats / by Karen Latchana Kenney.
Description: Minneapolis, MN: Jump!, Inc., [2018]
Series: Nature's superheroes | Audience: Ages 7-10.
Includes bibliographical references and index.
Identifiers: LCCN 2017032875 (print)
LCCN 2017032405 (ebook)
ISBN 9781624967108 (ebook)
ISBN 9781620319734 (hardcover: alk. paper)
ISBN 9781620319741 (pbk.)
Subjects: LCSH: Rats–Juvenile literature.
Classification: LCC QL737.R666 (print) | LCC QL737.
R666 K46 2017 (ebook) | DDC 599.35/2–dc23
LC record available at https://lccn.loc.gov/2017032875

Editor: Jenna Trnka
Book Designer: Michelle Sonnek
Photo Researcher: Michelle Sonnek

Photo Credits: Oleksandr Lysenko/Shutterstock, cover; Maslov Dmitry/Shutterstock, 1; Inara Prusakova/Shutterstock, 3; ericsphotography/iStock, 4; Nature Photographers Ltd/Alamy, 5; Gallinago_media/Shutterstock, 6-7; Antagain/iStock, 8 (rat), 16; Ammak/Shutterstock, 8 (block); blickwinkel/Alamy, 9; mammalpix/Alamy, 10-11; Dave Bevan/Alamy, 12-13; J.P. Ferrero & J.M. Labat/Biosphoto, 14-15; Biosphoto/SuperStock, 17; Derek Middleton/Minden Pictures/SuperStock, 18-19; PetStockBoys/Alamy, 20-21; Juniors/SuperStock, 23.

Printed in the United States of America at Corporate Graphics in North Mankato, Minnesota.

TABLE OF CONTENTS

CHAPTER 1

CLEVER RATS

What creatures can chew through concrete? What animals can feel with their whiskers? And what can crawl straight up a wall?

These creatures are smart. And they never give up. Their powers are incredible and surprising. They are rats!

There are 56 kinds of rats around the world. Rats are **rodents**. Some wild rats live by people and are pests. Wild rats also live in forests. They are smart animals. They use their powers to **survive** anywhere.

CHAPTER 2

SUPERHERO POWERS

No place is off-limits to rats. They are amazing climbers. They climb up walls and trees.

claw

tail

Rats scurry across wires and pipes. They grip with their sharp claws. Their long tails help them **balance**.

whiskers

Rats can't see very well. Instead they feel for things. But they don't use their paws. They use their long whiskers. Rats quickly brush these hairs against an object. They feel its size and shape. They locate where it is. Feeling helps rats see without their eyes.

How do rats hide from **predators**? They have a way of talking in secret. They send warning calls to other rats. The calls are too high for other animals to hear. Not even humans can hear the high sounds rats make.

DID YOU KNOW?

Rats also have super hearing. They hear sounds twice as high as what a dog can hear.

burrow

Rats move through forests. They find their way to food. And they return back to their **burrows**. How do they do this? They have an amazing **memory**. They learn and remember which way to go.

DID YOU KNOW?

Rats are very smart. Scientists have tested them. They can find their way through mazes. They can even be taught to catch a ball!

CHAPTER 3

CITY SMARTS

With their skills, rats can survive almost anywhere. They have **adapted** to city life and people. They live in **sewers** and buildings and under concrete slabs. How?

Rats are excellent swimmers. Some can swim for more than one mile (1.6 kilometers) at a time. They can also **tread** water for three days. This helps them survive in sewers and water.

A rat's front teeth never stop growing. But they don't get too long. This is because rats are super chewers. They chew through metal, plastic, and wood. This **grinds** their teeth down. Rats can even chew through concrete!

TAKE A LOOK!

A rat has many features that make it one of nature's superheroes!

EARS
Ears with sharp hearing help rats communicate with each other.

TAIL
A long tail helps a rat balance.

TEETH
Strong teeth help rats chew through just about anything.

CLAWS
Claws help rats grip and climb.

WHISKERS
Long whiskers feel objects and help rats understand their surroundings and find food.

Rats love living by people. People leave food out. Garbage bins are full of food scraps rats can eat. Meals are easy to find in the city. And in cities, rats have few predators. No matter where they are, rats use their super powers to survive.

DID YOU KNOW?

Female rats can **reproduce** every three weeks. This explains why some cities have a lot of rats!

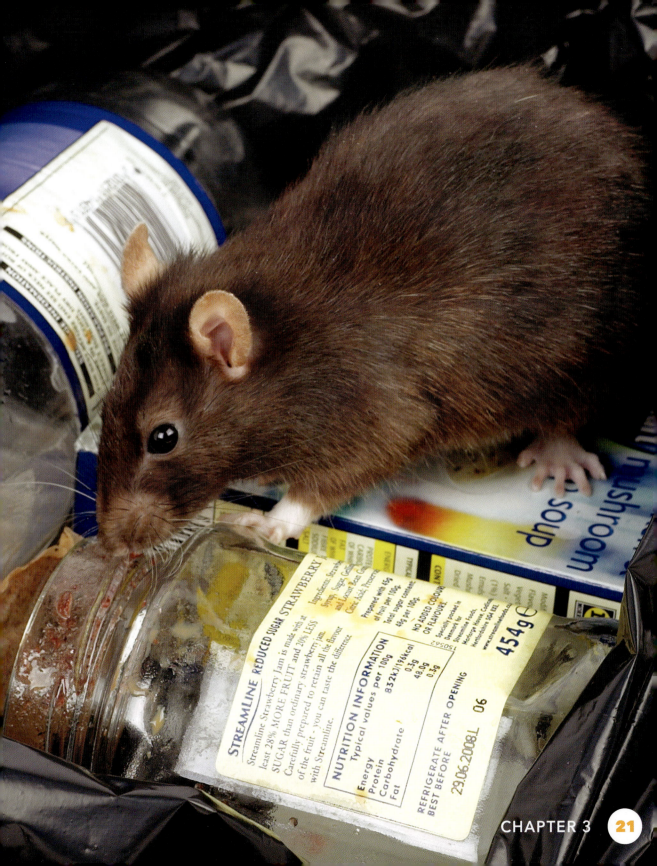

STREAMLINE REDUCED SUGAR STRAWBERRY
Streamline Strawberry Jam is made with at
least 28% MORE FRUIT and 20% LESS
SUGAR than ordinary strawberry jam.
Carefully prepared to retain all the flavour
of the fruit - you can taste the difference
with Streamline.

NUTRITION INFORMATION
Typical values per 100g
Energy   832kJ/194kcal
Protein   0.3g
Carbohydrate   48.0g
Fat   0.3g

REFRIGERATE AFTER OPENING
BEST BEFORE

29.06.2008L   06

454g ℮

ACTIVITIES & TOOLS

FEEL AND GUESS

Feel objects to guess what they are, just like rats do.

What You Need:
- partner
- blindfold
- mystery objects

❶ Ask a partner to pick three mystery objects for you to feel.

❷ Put on your blindfold. Ask your partner to hold an object in front of you.

❸ Touch the object quickly, just like a rat does with its whiskers. Don't hold the object.

❹ Is it:
- hard or soft?
- a certain shape?
- wet or dry?
- sticky or grainy?

❺ Now try to guess what the object is. How many guesses does it take?

❻ Try again with the other objects. Then switch so your partner can try with three new objects.

adapted: To have changed to live in a new situation.

balance: To stay steady and not fall.

burrows: Holes and tunnels in the ground that animals use.

grinds: Wears down.

memory: The ability to remember things.

predators: Animals that hunt other animals for food.

reproduce: To produce young.

rodents: Mammals with large front teeth that are used to gnaw on things.

sewers: Underground pipe systems that carry away liquid and solid waste.

survive: To continue to live.

tread: To swim in one place and keep the head above water.

INDEX

TO LEARN MORE

Learning more is as easy as 1, 2, 3.

1) Go to www.factsurfer.com

2) Enter "superrats" into the search box.

3) Click the "Surf" button to see a list of websites.

With factsurfer, finding more information is just a click away.